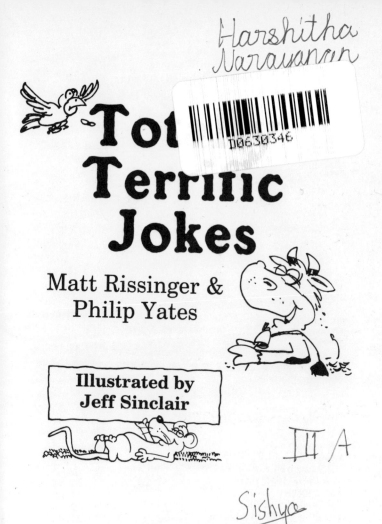

Totally Terrific Jokes

Matt Rissinger & Philip Yates

Illustrated by Jeff Sinclair

GOODWILL PUBLISHING HOUSE
B-3 Rattan jyoti,18 Rajendra Place
New Delhi-110008 (INDIA)

This special low priced Indian reprint is published by arrangement with Sterling Publishing Company, Inc. New York.

Published in India by
GOODWILL PUBLISHING HOUSE
B-3 Rattan jyoti,18 Rajendra Place
New Delhi-110008 (INDIA)
Tel. : 25750801, 25755519, 25820556
Fax : 91-11-25763428
E-mail : goodwillpub@vsnl.net
website : www.goodwillpublishinghouse.com

Printed at :-
Kumar offset
New Delhi

Contents

1. Jokes Galore and More!

What has no fingers but wears many rings?
A tree.

What kind of trees do fingers grow on?
Palm trees.

What grows on trees and is terrified of wolves?
The three little figs.

What do trees watch on television?
Their favorite sap operas.

Tɪᴘ: What's black and white and surrounded by red?

Tᴏᴘ: A Dalmatian on a fire truck.

What dogs watch stock car racing on TV?
Lap dogs.

Did you hear about the new cable channel for sports jocks with bad handwriting? It's called ESPNmanship.

"Doctor, doctor, I think I'm a VCR."
"Oh, why don't you just relax and rewind."

Why are pianos hard to open?
The keys are inside.

What keeps jazz musicians on earth?
Groovity.

A Scotsman arrived in New York and soon was set up in his own apartment. After a few weeks, his mother called to see how he was doing.

"Terrible!" replied the Scotsman. "All day long some crazy guy bangs on my wall and yells, 'I can't take it anymore! I can't take it anymore!' "

"I'm so sorry," said his mother.

"But that's not all," said the Scotsman. "On the other side some woman cries and moans all day long."

"Well, Son," advised his mother, "if I were you, I'd keep to myself."

"Oh, I do," replied the Scotsman. "I just sit in my room all day and play the bagpipes."

TONGUE TWISTERS
SAY THIS THREE TIMES QUICKLY...

A noisy noise annoys an oyster.

Nine nice night nurses nursing nicely

WILLY: What happens when you play a country song backwards?
BILLY: You get your dog back, your truck back, and your girlfriend back!

Why is Elvis so cool?
Because of all his fans.

TEX: What is the slowest mountain?
LEX: Mt. Everest.

LEX: What is the quickest mountain?
TEX: Mt. Rushmore.

Why don't mountains get cold in the winter?
Because they wear snow caps.

TOTALLY TERRIFIC JOKES

Where do computers go to dance?
To a disk-oteque.

Why did the computer squeak?
Because someone stepped on its mouse.

Did you hear about the computer for hunters?
When you turn it on it says, "You've got quail."

ZEKE: I'm writing a sci-fi book about a man with rabies stuck inside a computer.
FREAK: What are you calling it?
ZEKE: *The Foamer in the Dell.*

What would you call two Internet surfers who just got married?
Newlywebs.

JEN: How is the Internet like an overgrown yard?
LEN: You have to modem both.

Why did the elf want to get on the Internet?
So he could build a gnome page.

FRED: My computer is very hard on shoes.
NED: Why do you say that?
FRED: It keeps needing to be re-booted.

What did the tie say to the hat?
"You go on a head, I'll just hang around."

What did the pencil sharpener say to the pencil?
"Stop going in circles and get to the point."

What did the mail handling machine say to the
envelope?
Nothing, it was out of sorts.

An able-bodied seaman met a pirate and they took turns recounting their adventures at sea. Noting the pirate's pegleg, hook, and eye patch, the seaman asked, "So, how did you end up with the pegleg?"

"Well," said the pirate, "we was caught in a monster storm off the cape and a giant wave swept me overboard. Just as they were pullin' me out, a school of sharks appeared and one of 'em bit me leg off."

"Blimey!" exclaimed the seaman. "What about the hook?"

"Ahhhh," continued the pirate, "we were boardin' a trader ship, pistols blastin' and swords swingin' this way and that. Somehow I got me hand got chopped off."

"Zounds!" remarked the seaman. "And how came ye by the eye patch?"

"A seagull droppin' fell into me eye," answered the pirate.

"You lost your eye to a seagull dropping?" the sailor asked incredulously.

"Agh," said the pirate, "it was me first day with the hook."

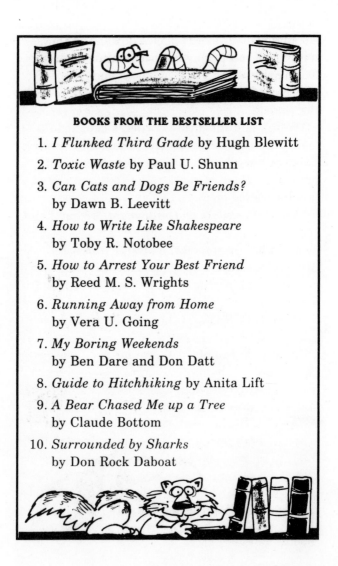

BOOKS FROM THE BESTSELLER LIST

1. *I Flunked Third Grade* by Hugh Blewitt

2. *Toxic Waste* by Paul U. Shunn

3. *Can Cats and Dogs Be Friends?*
   by Dawn B. Leevitt

4. *How to Write Like Shakespeare*
   by Toby R. Notobee

5. *How to Arrest Your Best Friend*
   by Reed M. S. Wrights

6. *Running Away from Home*
   by Vera U. Going

7. *My Boring Weekends*
   by Ben Dare and Don Datt

8. *Guide to Hitchhiking* by Anita Lift

9. *A Bear Chased Me up a Tree*
   by Claude Bottom

10. *Surrounded by Sharks*
    by Don Rock Daboat

Tip and Top had never played Trivial Pursuit before and both looked baffled when Tip landed on "Science and Nature."

"If you are in a vacuum," Top read the question, "and someone calls your name, can you hear it?"

Thinking hard for a second, Tip finally replied, "Depends on whether the vacuum is on or off, doesn't it?"

Motto for clones: "To thine own self be two."

CHICKIE: How do you blow up a balloon?
DICKIE: Try poking it with a sharp pencil.

Why did the balloon burst?
Because it saw the lollipop!

LOU: Did you hear about the boatload of plastic building toys that sank in the ocean?

STU: Wow, talk about 20,000 Legos Under the Sea!

HARRY: Did you hear about the boatload of shoes that sunk in the Atlantic?

LARRY: No, what happened?

Harry: 300 soles were lost at sea.

How do shells get to the beach?
They take the shellevator.

PATIENT: Doctor, I have yellow teeth, what should I do?

DENTIST: Wear a brown tie.

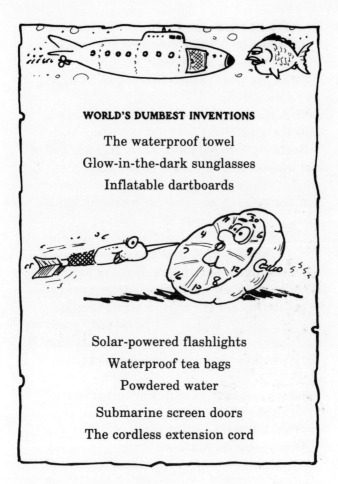

WORLD'S DUMBEST INVENTIONS

The waterproof towel

Glow-in-the-dark sunglasses

Inflatable dartboards

Solar-powered flashlights

Waterproof tea bags

Powdered water

Submarine screen doors

The cordless extension cord

VINNY: How do you park a computer?
GINNY: First, you back it up...

One day Howard was driving to the lake for a swim when he noticed a man on the side of the highway dressed all in red.

"Who are you?" asked Howard as he pulled up to the stranger.

"I'm the Man in Red and I'm very hungry," said the man.

Reaching into his lunch sack, Howard pulled out a sandwich, handed it to the man, then sped off down the road.

A few miles later, Howard spotted another man, this time dressed all in yellow.

"What can I do for you?" asked Howard.

"I'm the Man in Yellow and I'm very thirsty."

Pulling out a can of soda, Howard handed the Coke to the man, then resumed his journey.

Anxious to get to the lake before sunset, Howard put his foot to the pedal and roared off down the road, only to spot yet another man, dressed all in blue, signaling for Howard to stop.

"Don't tell me!" said Howard impatiently. "You're the Man in Blue, right?"

"That's right!" replied the man.

"Well, what do you want?"

"Driver's license and registration, please."

Why did the first hand cross the street?
To get to the second hand shop.

HOW DO THEY TRAVEL?

Frogs hop a plane.

Hens fly the coop.

Snakes slide home.

Kangaroos jump ship.

Worms crawl a cab.

MOLLY: How do you know there's a cannibal family next door?

DOLLY: In their driveway are empty pizza vans and full pizza boxes.

What did the cannibals say when a baseball team washed up on shore?

"Look—a nine-corpse meal."

What would cannibals say if they saw two campers in sleeping bags?

"Breakfast in bed."

Cannibal Airlines:
Check out our Frequent Fryer Miles

2. Crime and Pun-ishment!

JASON: The bullies at my school are so tough they eat sardines.

MASON: What's so tough about that?

JASON: Without opening the can?

Did you hear about the dweeb who kept a stick of dynamite in his car's emergency repair kit? He figured if he got a flat he could blow up his tires.

> **SIGN AT A CAR DEALERSHIP**
> The best way to get back on your feet—
> miss a car payment.

WILLIE: My uncle started out life as an unwanted child.

DILLIE: Have things changed?

WILLIE: You bet. Now he's wanted in fifty states.

ART TEACHER: What did you draw?

MASON: A cop chasing a robber.

ART TEACHER: But I don't see any robber.

MASON: That's because he got away.

"Well," said the judge to the bank robber after the verdict had been read. "Now that you've been found not guilty, you are free to go."

"Hooray!" said the bank robber. "But I have one question, Judge."

"What's that?"

"Does this mean I have to give the money back?"

"Trick or treat!" said the boy dressed in a Buzz Light Year Space Suit.

"Who are you supposed to be?" asked the man.

"I'm from *Toy Story*!" replied the boy, grabbing a handful of candy and running down the street.

A few minutes later there was another knock on the door.

"Trick or treat!" said the same boy.

"Who are you supposed to be now," asked the man crankily, "*Toy Story II?*"

With that, he grabbed the kid's trick or treat sack and slammed the door.

"Who was that?" asked the boy's friend.

"Who do you think?" said the boy. "Terminator III."

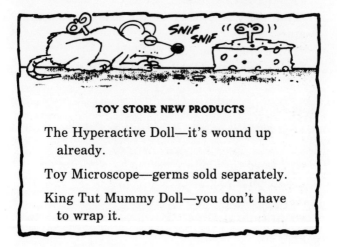

TOY STORE NEW PRODUCTS

The Hyperactive Doll—it's wound up already.

Toy Microscope—germs sold separately.

King Tut Mummy Doll—you don't have to wrap it.

POLICE CAPTAIN: Did you hear about the theft of 100 blankets at the city hospital?
SERGEANT: No.
POLICE CAPTAIN: Just as I thought—a cover-up.

Why would Snow White make a great judge?
Because she's the fairest of them all.

A woman suspected someone was stealing her loose change at home. She set up a hidden camera but the only one on the tape was her cat. She took the cat to the doctor, who made an X-ray. The doctor came back and said, "I have good news and bad news."

"What's the bad news? asked the woman.

"Your cat has unusual eating habits," said the doctor.

"Then what's the good news?"

"The good news is there's money in the kitty."

Why did the cannibals cook the crook?
They wanted to take a bite out of crime.

NAT: I tried to calm my nerves by working on jigsaw puzzles.
PAT: Did it work?
NAT: Are you kidding? My whole life is going to pieces.

What do you call a bug that arrests other bugs?
  A cop-roach.

When the news photographer heard about the
forest fire, he hired a plane so he could snap
pictures from the air. Arriving at the airport, the
photographer jumped into the plane, and within
seconds the aircraft had taken off.

"Can you get any closer to the fire?" asked the
photographer.

"Why should I do that?" said the pilot.

"Because I want to get pictures for the
newspaper."

"You mean you're not the flight instructor?"
gulped the pilot.

DILLY: What happened to Frankenstein when he was caught speeding?

DALLY: He was fined $50 and dismantled for six months.

FRANKLY SON, WHERE ARE YOUR BRAINS?

"Your Honor," said the smartest lawyer in the world, "my client is not guilty. He merely inserted his arm into a window and stole some jewelry. His arm is not himself. I fail to see how you can punish the whole individual for an offense committed by one arm."

"I agree," nodded the judge. "I hereby sentence the defendant's arm to one year in prison. He may accompany the arm or not."

"Thank you, Your Honor," said the defendant as he detached his artificial limb, laid it on the bench, and walked out.

Did you hear about the turtle that was mugged by a snail? When the police asked for a description of the suspect, the turtle replied, "I don't know. It all happened so fast..."

"I have good news and bad news," said the lawyer to his client. "The bad news is your blood test came back, and your DNA is an exact match with that found at the crime scene."

"Oh, no!" cried the client. "What's the good news?"

"The good news is your cholesterol is down to 140."

Who was the world's first ever underwater spy?
James Pond.

Did you hear about the crook who tried to hijack a busload of tourists? The police have 2,000 photographs of the suspect.

Police examiner to rookie: "What would you do if you had to arrest your own mother?"

"First, I'd call for backup..."

What would you get if you crossed a chicken and a robber?
A peck-pocket.

A burglar broke into a house one night. Shining his flashlight on the floor in the dark, he heard a voice saying, "God is watching you."

Looking around nervously, he shook his head and continued to search for valuables.

"God is watching you!" came the voice again.

This time the burglar shone his flashlight on a parrot. "Did you say that?" said the burglar to the bird.

"Yes, I did," squawked the parrot. "My name is Moses."

"What kind of stupid people would name their parrot 'Moses,'" laughed the burglar.

Suddenly, behind the burglar there was a low growling noise.

"Squawk!" said the parrot. "The same people who would name a pit bull 'God.'"

What happened when the duck was arrested?
He quacked under pressure.

Why did the cop give Godzilla a ticket?
He ran through a stomp sign.

Why did the dog get a ticket?
For double-barking.

TRIXIE: Is it true your mom drives too fast?
DIXIE: Are you kidding? She got stopped for
speeding so many times the police gave her
season tickets.

Leonard was not the brightest man in town, but when he heard the local sheriff was looking for a deputy, Leonard decided he was right for the job.

"Before I hire you, I want you to answer some questions," said the sheriff. "What is 1 and 1?"

Thinking long and hard, Leonard finally answered, "11."

"Well, that's not what I meant," said the sheriff. "But I guess you're right. Okay, what two days of the week start with the letter T?"

"That would be today and tomorrow," said Leonard.

"Well, that's not what I meant, but I guess you're right. Now here's the last question—who killed Abraham Lincoln?"

"I don't know," said Leonard, looking confused.

"Well, why don't you go home and think about that one."

That night Leonard went home and told his mother about the interview. "It went great," said Leonard excitedly. "First day on the job and already I'm working on a murder case!"

3. Fiendishly Funny!

What was King Tut's favorite card game?
Gin Mummy.

What is a mummy's favorite treat?
Cotton candy.

How do you tell when a mummy is sick?
He's all stuffed up.

PATIENT: Doctor I think I'm a mummy. What do you think?
DOCTOR: I don't think you're wrapped too tight.

Mummy movie producer to director:
"Is the film finished yet?"
"No, I still have a few loose ends to tie up."

What kind of underwear do mummies wear?
Fruit of the Tomb.

Where would you find a life-size figure of Lizzie Borden?
At a whacks museum.

What's big, hairy, and has a pen between his toes?
Bic-foot.

What would you get if you crossed a snake with Bigfoot?
Sssssss-quatch.

Where do baby monsters go when their parents
are at work?
  Day-scare centers.

What's a monster's favorite play?
  Romeo and Ghouliet.

Who is the best dancer at a monster party?
  The Boogie Man.

Why do most monsters have wrinkles?
  Have you ever tried to iron a monster?

Where did the monster keep her extra fingers?
  In her handbag.

What do witches wear to bed?
Fright-gowns.

What kind of underwear do witches wear?
Fruit of the Broom.

Why don't witches ride their brooms when they're angry?
They might fly off the handle.

How many witches does it take to change a light-bulb?
Just one, but she changes it into a toad.

What kind of prize do the best witches get?
Academy A-warts.

How do you communicate with the Loch Ness Monster at 20,000 fathoms?
Drop her a line.

BABY DRAGON: Mommy, Mommy I had a terrible dream where a guy in a tin suit was chasing me with a sword!
MOMMY DRAGON: There, there, dear—that was just a knightmare.

BEN: On what planet would you find the most trash?
KEN: Pollute-o.

How can you tell that Martians are good gardeners?
They have a little green thumb.

What did the Martian say when he landed in a flower bed?
"Take me to your weeder."

What did the traffic-light say to the Martian?
"Don't look now, I'm changing!"

What protozoa likes Halloween?
An amoe-boo!

What would you get if you crossed a skunk with Frankenstein?
Stankenstein.

What is Frankenstein's favorite movie?
Scar Wars.

What *Star Wars* villain disappeared into thin air?
Darth Vapor.

Why are dinosaurs healthier than dragons?
Because dinosaurs don't smoke.

Why did the vampire cross the road?
  Because he was attached to the chicken's neck.

What do they feed vampires for their last meal?
  Stake and potatoes.

Who is Dracula most likely to fall in love with?
  The girl necks door.

What would you get if you crossed a vampire and a snowman?
  Frostbite.

Why didn't the vampire suck your blood?
  He was on his coffin break.

What would you get if you crossed a beautiful model with a ghost?
  A cover ghoul.

What would you get if you crossed a ghost with a pair of trousers?
  Scaredy pants.

What would you get if you crossed a ghost with an anteater?
  A phantom that loves picnics.

What happened when the tree saw the ghost?
  It was petrified.

What do shortsighted ghosts wear?
Spookacles!

What do ghosts order when they go to a Chinese restaurant?
Fright rice.

What's a ghost's favorite exercise machine?
The scare-master.

What did the baby zombie want for his birthday?
A deady bear.

Have you ever seen the Abominable Snowman?
No, not yeti.

SIGN AT A FUNERAL HOME:
"Drive carefully, we'll wait."

How do serial killers travel through the forest?
They take the psycho path.

What long-necked dinosaur loved classical music?
Bach-iosaurus.

How do you raise an orphaned Tyrannosaurus?
With a front-end loader.

What would you get if you crossed the Easter Bunny and a parrot?
A rabbit that tells where it hid the eggs.

What would you get if you crossed a pig with the principal?
Expelled.

What big gorilla fell into a cement mixer?
King Kong-crete.

What do farm kids say on Halloween?
"Tractor Treat!"

Where does Dracula tell ghost stories?
Around the vamp-fire.

What is a ghoul's favorite cheese?
Monsterella.

What is ghoul's favorite amusement park ride?
The roller-ghoster.

Why doesn't a skeleton play music in a church?
Because it has no organs!

Why didn't the skeleton go to the ball?
Because he had no body to go with.

What is a skeleton's favorite instrument?
A trom-bone.

What did the skeleton say while riding his
Harley?
"Bone to be wild!"

4. On Your Mark...Get Set...Laugh!

What game did Godzilla play with people?
Squash.

What can lizards do that snakes can't do?
Stretch their legs.

What's big and gray and weighs down the front of your car?
An elephant in the glove compartment.

Did you hear about the track star that raced a rabbit?

He won by a hare.

JILL: Never tell a joke while you're ice-skating.
PHIL: Why not?
JILL: Because the ice might crack up.

What's the difference between a boxer and a computer program?

One's a bruiser, one's a browser.

What would you get if you crossed a computer with a fast car?

A click and drag race.

What can you serve but never eat?

A volleyball.

What kind of socks do baseball players like?
Ones with lots of runs in them.

TONGUE TWISTERS
SAY THIS THREE TIMES QUICKLY...

Short spotted socks.
Shy Shelly says she shall
sew sheets.

Why did the bungee jumper take a vacation?
Because he was at the end of his rope.

Why did the skeleton refuse to bungee jump?
He didn't have the guts.

Why did the skeleton cross the road?
To get to the Body Shop!

What would you get if you crossed a boomerang
with a bad memory?
I don't know, but it'll come back to me.

Where did Noah keep the pinball machine?
In the Ark-ade.

"Your teacher said I can't let you play football," said Andy's coach, "until you improve your math skills."

"All right," said Andy, "ask me anything."

"What is two plus two?"

Thinking hard for a moment, Andy answered, "Two plus two is four."

"Did you say four?" said the coach excitedly. "Did you say four?"

Just then the other players on the team piped in, "Come on, coach, give him another chance!"

What do you call a football player who keeps giving up?
A quitter-back.

What position did the ghost play on the hockey team?
Ghoulie.

What is it called when nudists jump rope?
Skippy dipping.

Why don't elephants like to ride bicycles?
Because they prefer vehicles with a trunk.

MIA: Can two elephants go swimming?
TIA: Are you kidding? With one pair of trunks!

What do you call a skunk that excels at basketball?

A slam dunk skunk.

What is a mummy's favorite sport?

Casketball!

What do you call a dinosaur that lifts weights?

Tyrannosaurus Pecs.

WHEW! I'M GETTING DINO SORE!

What would you get if you crossed boomerangs with bad Christmas presents?

Gifts that return themselves.

Why did the tennis coach give his team a lighter?

Because they kept losing their matches!

JERRY: I just can't train my dog to hit home runs.
TERRY: Why not?
JERRY: Because he prefers being walked.

What would you get if you crossed an evil crone with a curve ball?
The Wicked Pitch of the West.

One day a fisherman realized he had forgotten his bait. Spotting a frog with a worm in its mouth, he grabbed the frog and yanked the worm out. As a reward, he popped a candy bar into the frog's mouth.

A few minutes later, he felt a tug on his boot. When he looked down, he saw the same frog, but this time with three worms in its mouth.

What would you get if you crossed a bronco with a dog?
An animal whose buck is worse than his bite.

5. Kid Crack-Ups!

WILL: What do you call a kid with a lightbulb in his head?

DILL: Pretty bright.

A Sunday school teacher was teaching her students about a higher power.

"Hey, look!" said Matthew, holding up a piece of paper. "Look what I spelled."

Glancing down at Matthew's paper, the teacher saw the word 'GOD' neatly spelled out.

"That's very good, Matthew! Now what does that say?"

"I'm not done yet," said Matthew. "How do you spell 'ZILLA'?"

STU: My dad's car is pretty old.
LOU: How old is it?
STU: It's so old, the license plates are in Roman numerals.

CLARA: Did you hear the Queen burped in public?
SARA: Yes, but I hear she issued a royal pardon.

What didn't King Arthur ever get served at the Round Table?
A square meal.

MUST BE CHICKEN KNIGHT!

Who looks through your window and never wants to grow up?
Peeper Pan.

One day Hubert discovered a bottle buried in the sand. When he rubbed it, a genie appeared and said, "I grant you three wishes."

"I want to be the richest man on earth," said Hubert.

A puff of smoke rose in the air and soon the entire beach was covered with millions of gold coins!

"Next," said Hubert thoughtfully, "I want a body just like Arnold Schwarzenegger's."

Another puff of smoke and suddenly Hubert had the finest muscles ever seen on a man.

"Finally," Hubert smiled, "for my last wish I want to be irresistible to girls."

One final puff of smoke and zap! Hubert turned into a Barbie Doll.

LEM: You're a promising singer.
CLEM: Really?
LEM: Yes, in fact, you should promise to stop singing.

DAD: Why did you get kicked out of summer camp?
CHAD: For being a responsible camper!
DAD: And what were you responsible for?
CHAD: For flying the counselor's underwear from the flagpole.

VERN: Our new house is pretty big.
FERN: How big is it?
VERN: It's so big the bathtub has a diving board.

JAN: Why are you putting lipstick on your forehead?
NAN: I'm just tryuing to make up my mind.

TIFFANY: Mom, can I go outside and play with the boys?
MOM: No, you can't play with the boys—they're too rough.
TIFFANY: If I find a smooth one, can I play with him?

He's so absent-minded he hides his own Easter eggs.

He's so dumb he thinks barnacles are places where sea horses live.

> He's so rich, when he cashed a check at the bank, the bank bounced.

GOMER: What has four legs, is big, green, and fuzzy, and if it fell out of a tree, would kill you?
HOMER: I have no idea.
GOMER: A pool table.

CHAD: My family lives in a nudist colony.
BRAD: Gee, I bet that takes all the fun out of Halloween.

How can you put your left hand in your right pocket and your right hand in your left pocket without crossing your hands?
Put your pants on backwards.

Little Jimmy came home from a birthday party, waving his door prize excitedly at his mother. "Look what I won, Mom!"

"Why, it's a thermos," said Jimmy's mother.

"What's a thermos?" said Jimmy.

"A thermos keeps hot things hot and cold things cold."

The next morning Jimmy packed his lunch and was about to leave for school when his mother stopped him. "Jimmy, what did you pack for lunch?

"Don't worry, mom, I have it all in my thermos."

"What did you put in there?"

"A cup of soup and a popsicle."

IGGY: What is the height of stupidity?
ZIGGY: I don't know, how tall are you?

Bratty Clint and his sister went to the fair and found a nickel scale that tells your fortune and weight.

"Hey, listen to this," said Clint, showing his sister a small white card. "It says I'm bright, energetic, and a great brother."

"Yeah," Clint's sister nodded, "and it has your weight wrong, too."

DILL: Last night my sister and I had an argument, but it ended when she came crawling to me on her hands and knees.

WILL: What did she say?

DILL: She said, "Come out from under that bed, you coward!"

"Son, why did you tattoo numbers all over your body?"

"That's so you can always count on me, Dad."

DILLY: How do you spot a dweeb at the airport?

DALLY: He's the one throwing bread to the planes.

What kind of car does Luke Skywalker drive?
A Toy-Yoda.

Why did Luke Skywalker always sleep with the light on?
He was afraid of the Darth.

MOM: Lenny, did you wake up grumpy this morning?
LENNY: No, I think Dad woke himself up.

Where do baby Vikings go when their parents are at work?
To the Norse-ery.

FRANK: How is your new girlfriend?
TANK: She's like a prizefighter.
FRANK: You mean she's a real knockout?
TANK: No, I mean she spits and sweats a lot.

KID 1: My dad can crack a twenty-pound board with just his hand.
KID 2: That's nothing. My dad can crack a 1,000-pound safe with just his fingers.

One day Milton asked his father to buy him a set of weightlifting equipment. "I want to look like Arnold Schwarzenegger," said Milton. "Please?"

"All right," said Milton's father. "But you have to promise to use them every day."

That day at the sporting goods store, Milton and his father picked out a set of weights and a bench press.

"Are you sure about this?" asked Milton's father.

"Please, Dad," said Milton. "I want to build up my muscles."

"Okay," said Milton's father when he had finished paying. "Let's get this home."

"You've got to be kidding, Dad," said Milton. "Do you expect me to carry this stuff to the car?"

What would you get if you crossed a groundhog and a school bully?
Six more weeks of detention.

FLOYD: I wanted to go fishing with my dad, but he told me school was more important.
TEACHER: And did he tell you why school is more important?
FLOYD: Yes, because he didn't have enough bait for the both of us.

PRINCIPAL: Why are you late to school?
CLASS CLOWN: I sprained my leg skateboarding.
PRINCIPAL: That's a lame excuse.

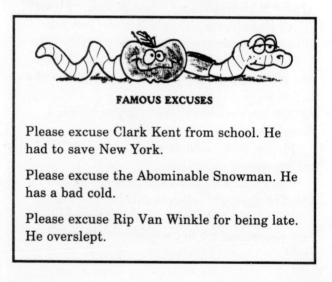

FAMOUS EXCUSES

Please excuse Clark Kent from school. He had to save New York.

Please excuse the Abominable Snowman. He has a bad cold.

Please excuse Rip Van Winkle for being late. He overslept.

TEACHER: Slim, please use the word "canoe" in a sentence.

SLIM: Canoe repeat that?

TEACHER: Tanya, please use the word "mariner" in a sentence.

TANYA: My brother has a girlfriend and he's planning on mariner.

To encourage all his students to become smarter, the principal at a grade school hung a sign above the bathroom sink with one word on it—"THINK!"

The next day somebody hung another sign above the detergent dispenser saying, "THOAP!"

6. Pet Jest!

"Look, Mom!" said Billy when he and his mother arrived at the little country store. Posted on the glass door was a sign saying, "Danger! Beware of Dog!"

Carefully, Billy and his mom entered the store, only to find a harmless old hound dog asleep on the floor.

"Is that the dog we're supposed to be afraid of?" said Billy to the storeowner.

"That's him," replied the storeowner.

"He doesn't look dangerous to me," said Billy. "Why did you hang that sign?"

"Because," said the owner, "before I hung that sign up, people kept tripping over him."

Two birds watched as a turtle took two hours to climb a tree, then perched on a branch and jumped off, crashing straight to the ground.

Uninjured, the turtle began the long climb up the tree again, jumped, and fell to the ground.

"Honey," said the first bird to the second, "don't you think it's time we told Morris he's adopted?"

What do you call a frog with no back legs?
Unhoppy!

What happens when a frog is double-parked on a lily pad?
It's toad away.

"Mommy! Mommy!" cried Gerald when he and his Dad got home from the pet shop.

"We saw a litter of kittens. There were two boy kittens and two girl kittens."

"How did you know that?" his mother asked.

"Because Daddy picked them up and looked underneath," he replied. "Which means there had to be a sticker on the bottom."

DANA: How do you know when your cat's been on the Internet?

LANA: Your mouse has teeth marks in it.

What do you call a cat with a pager?
A beeping tom.

CALLING ALL CATS!.. TUNA TRUCK OVERTURNED 4TH AND MAIN!

What do baby cats wear?

Diapurrrrs.

A man was driving along the highway when a rabbit suddenly jumped in front of him. Getting out of the car, he examined the poor animal, which seemed to be dead.

Just then a truck pulled up and a woman stepped out.

"Don't you worry," said the woman, pulling a spray can from her glove compartment.

She sprayed the contents of the can onto the rabbit. As the man watched, the rabbit twitched its nose and came to life. Leaping to its feet, it waved its paw at the humans, hopped down the road, stopped, waved again, then continued down the road, stopping and waving every few feet.

"That was amazing!" said the man. "What was in that can?"

"See for yourself," the woman smiled.

The man read the label on the spray can: "Hare Spray. Restores Life to Dead Hare. Adds Permanent Wave."

What would you get if you crossed a shark with a parrot?

A fish that talks your head off.

A woman in a butcher shop spotted a dog waiting at the counter.

"How much ground beef do you need today?" said the butcher to the dog. The dog barked twice and with that, the butcher wrapped up two pounds of ground beef.

"How many pork chops today?" said the butcher. The dog barked four times and the butcher wrapped up four pork chops.

Grabbing the packages in his mouth, the dog headed out the door and trotted down the street. Curious, the woman followed the dog to an apartment house and watched as the animal pressed the doorbell with his nose.

When an old man opened the door, the woman remarked to the owner, "You sure have a smart dog there."

"Smart? Are you kidding?" said the old man. "This is the third time this week he forgot his key."

What's black and white and red all over?
A zebra with zits!

What did the rooster say when he saw Humpty Dumpty fall?
"Crack-a-doodle-doo."

How did the pig store his computer files?
  On sloppy disks!

What do you give a dog that loves computers?
  Doggy diskettes.

My dog is so computer savvy, the other day I caught him logged onto the traffic network chasing virtual cars.

What animal would you like to be on a cold day?
  A little otter.

What is a snake's favorite subject?
  Sssssscience.

Where do eagles do most of their shopping?
At the swooper market.

What kind of animal has a bill in his name but none on his face?
A ger-bill.

What Arctic bird lives in a bakery?
A cream puffin.

Where do endangered birds live?
In condor-miniums.

What insect keeps good time?
A clock-roach.

One day, a baby camel asked his mother, "Mom, why have I got these huge three-toed feet?"

"Well, Son," replied the camel's mother, "that's so when we walk across the desert our toes will help us stay on top of the soft sand."

"Mom, why have I got these long eyelashes?" asked the baby camel.

"Because our eyelashes keep the sand out of our eyes on those long trips through the desert."

"Okay, then, why have I got these great big humps on my back?"

"They are there to help us store fat for our long treks across the desert. That way we can go without water for long periods."

"So," said the baby camel, "we have huge toes to protect our feet, long eyelashes to keep the sand out of our eyes, and big humps to store water?"

"That's right," said the camel's mother, impatiently. "Is there anything else you'd like to know?"

"Just one thing, Mom," said the baby camel. "What the heck are we doing in the San Diego Zoo?"

What would you get if you crossed a monkey with powdered orange juice?
An Oranga-Tang.

ANIMAL ACCEPTANCE SPEECHES

GIRAFFE: Thanks to all the people who stuck their necks out for me."

DALMATIAN: "I want to thank the casting director who first spotted me."

BLACK STALLION: "I want to thank my fodder."

LITTLE BO PEEP: "I couldn't have done it without ewe."

FREE WILLY: "I want to tank all my friends."

VAMPIRE BAT: "I want to thank everyone who hung around for me."

POLLY PARROT: "I'm speechless."

KING KONG: "The movie and this award have taken my career to new heights."

Why didn't Stuart Little win an Academy Award?

Because Mice Guys Finish Last.

What's big and gray and weighs down the front of your car?

An elephant disguised as a hood ornament.

SAMMY: What's the difference between an Asian elephant and an African elephant?

TAMMY: About 3,000 miles.

Why aren't elephants welcome on nude beaches?

Because they won't take off their trunks.

Why do elephants lie on their backs?

To trip low-flying canaries.

Why do elephants wear sneakers in hotels?
So they won't wake up the other guests.

Joshua got a pony for his birthday. One day
Joshua went out to the barn and saw that some
bluejays had built a nest on the horse's back. He
called the animal control department and they
suggested that Joshua rub some yeast on the
pony's back and the birds would disappear.
Joshua did as he was told and, sure enough, the
next morning the birds were gone.

Moral: Yeast is yeast, and nest is nest, and
never the mane shall tweet.

Why don't fish like to go on-line?
Because they're afraid of getting caught in the Net.

What magazine do fish like to read?
Buoy's Life.

What did the fish say when it swam into a concrete wall?
"Dam."

What animal goes "Baa-Baa-Woof?"
A sheepdog.

Did you hear about the man who had a heart transplant from a sheep? When the doctor asked how he felt after the operation, the man replied, "Not Baaaaaaaaad!"

BEN: What do you call a turtle with propellers?
LEN: A shellicopter.

What did the snail say when he hitched a ride on the turtle's back?
"Whhhhhhhhhhheeeeeeeeeeeeeeeeeeeeeeeeee!!!"

7. Suture Self!

What four letters of the alphabet mean it's time to go to the dentist?

ICDK (I see decay)!

DENTIST: I'll pull your aching tooth out in five minutes.

PATIENT: How much will it cost?

DENTIST: One hundred dollars.

PATIENT: That much for just five minutes?

DENTIST: Well, if you prefer, I can pull it out very slowly.

A father was having a hard time getting his son to the dentist. He finally pulled him yelling into the office. The father picked up his son, put him in the chair, and sat down to read a magazine. Before he got it open, he heard a scream. Losing his temper, the father yelled, "What's going on?" An older voice cried out, "He bit my finger!"

My cousin is so skinny her dentist tells her to eat between brushing.

What can you say about a depressed dentist?
That he's down in the mouth.

What do you give a lemon when it's hurt?
Lemon-aid.

How do you revive a butterfly?
Moth-to-moth resuscitation.

How do you know what a snake is allergic to?
It depends on his medical hiss-tory.

Why did the tree go to the hospital?
For a sap-pendectomy.

Why did the Christmas tree go to the hospital?
It had tinsel-itis.

PATIENT: Doctor, you've got to help me. Some mornings I wake up and think I'm Donald Duck; other mornings I think I'm Mickey Mouse.

DOCTOR: Hmmm, how long have you been having these Disney spells?

"Doctor, doctor, I think I'm a pretzel."

"Don't worry, I'll straighten you out in no time."

"Doctor, Doctor, I keep thinking I'm a $10 bill."

"Go shopping—the change will do you good."

Three absent-minded professors went to the doctor for a memory test. The doctor asked the first professor, "What's three times three?"

"278," replied the first professor.

"What's three times three?" the doctor asked the second professor.

"Saturday," replied the second professor.

"What's three times three?" the doctor asked the third professor.

"Three times three is nine," said the third professor.

"That's great!" said the doctor. "How did you figure it out?"

"It was easy," replied the professor. "I simply subtracted 278 from Saturday."

When the plumber arrived at Doctor Mackie's house, there was water all over the floor. Unpacking his tools, the plumber set to work on the broken pipe and within a few minutes handed the doctor a bill for $600.

"$600!" exclaimed the doctor. "This is ridiculous! I don't even make that much as a doctor."

"Neither did I when I was a doctor," smiled the plumber.

Why did the computer go to the eye doctor?
To improve its web sight.

FLOYD: Doctor, Doctor, everyone thinks I'm a liar.
DOCTOR: I find that hard to believe.

What does a dentist call his X-rays?
Tooth-pics.

What kind of X-rays do foot doctors take?
Foot-ographs.

PATIENT: Doctor, I think I'm a goldfish. What
should I do?
DOCTOR: Here, take this tank-quilizer.

PATIENT: Doctor, I just swallowed some little
blue, green, and orange glass balls!
DOCTOR: How do you feel?
PATIENT: Marbleous!

"Doctor, Doctor, I think I'm a frog."
"Stick out your tongue."
"And say 'Ahh'?"
"No, I want you to get rid of that fly."

DOCTOR: Keep taking your medicine and you'll
live to be a hundred.
PATIENT: Doc, I'll be a hundred next Wednesday.
DOCTOR: In that case, stop taking the medicine
Thursday.

What bright bug is difficult to handle?
  A three-alarm firefly.

One night Clem's wife went into labor and the
doctor was called to help with the delivery. Since
there was no electricity, the doctor handed Clem
a lantern and said, "Hold this high so I can see
what I'm doing."
  Before long a baby girl arrived.
  "Wait a minute!" said the doctor. "Don't lower
the lantern yet. I think there's another."
  A moment later the doctor had delivered a
second baby, this time a boy.
  "Hold on!" cried the doctor a third time.
"There's another one coming."
  "Holy cow, Doc!" said Clem as he raised the
lantern again. "Do you think it's the light that's
attracting them?"

What pink stomach medicine do farmers give to
sick chicks?
  Peep-to-Bismol.

THINGS YOU DON'T WANT TO HEAR ON THE OPERATING TABLE

Oops!

Has anyone seen my watch?

Darn! Page 47 of the manual is missing!

Well, this book doesn't say that. What edition is your manual?

Come back with that! Bad dog!

Wait a minute, if this is his spleen, then what's that?

Hand me that...uh...that...uh...thingie...

If I can just remember how they did this on TV last week...

Oh, no, there go the lights again.

Everybody stand back! I lost my contact lens!

I wish I hadn't forgotten my glasses.

Sterile, shmerile. The floor's clean, right?

I don't know what it is, but hurry up and pack it in ice.

TOTALLY TERRIFIC JOKES

Killer whale to son: "It's time you got braces for your teeth."

"Oh, do I have to go to the orca-dontist?

When Luther came down with a bad case of the flu, he called his doctor for an appointment.

"The doctor can see you in three weeks," said the receptionist.

"Three weeks?" exclaimed Luther. "I might be dead in three weeks!"

"If that happens," replied the receptionist, "would you do us a favor and have someone call to cancel the appointment?"

While Hubert waited to see his doctor, he heard a voice shout from behind the wall, "Measles! Typhoid! Tetanus!"

"Doctor, is the nurse all right?" said Hubert to his doctor.

"Oh, don't worry about her," replied the doctor. "She just likes to call the shots around here."

Doctor to patient: "I have good news and bad news. The bad news is you have a terrible, horrible new unnamed disease."

"What's the good news?"

"The good news is I get to name the disease after me and become horribly rich and terribly famous."

PATIENT: Yesterday I thought I was a pig.
DOCTOR: How are you today?
PATIENT: Swine, thanks!

8. Knock-Knock-ularity!

Knock-knock!
  Who's there?
Agatha.
  Agatha who?
Agatha feeling you
don't like me.

Knock-knock!
  Who's there?
Carfare.
  Carfare who?
Carfare a banana?

Knock-knock!
  Who's there?
Buttenut who?
  Butternut who?
Butternut try to fool
with me.

Knock-knock!
  Who's there?
Closure.
  Closure who?
Closure mouth when
you eat!

Knock-knock!
  Who's there?
Divan.
  Divan who?
Divan the bathtub and you'll hurt your head.

  Knock-knock!
    Who's there?
  Distress?
    Distress who?
  Distress looks nice with dem shoes.

    Knock-knock!
      Who's there?
    Emerson.
      Emerson who?
    Emerson ugly shoes!

Knock-knock!
  Who's there?
Dozen.
  Dozen who?
Dozen look like rain.

        Knock-knock!
          Who's there?
        Four E's.
          Four E's who?
        Four E's a jolly good fellow…!

Knock-knock!
  Who's there?
Josh.
  Josh who?
Josh you wait!

Knock-knock!
  Who's there?
Lettuce.
  Lettuce who?
Lettuce be a lesson to you!

Knock-knock!
  Who's there?
Lois.
  Lois who?
I got the Lois grade in the class.

Knock-knock!
  Who's there?
Marcella.
  Marcella who?
Marcella's full of water and I'm drowning!

Knock-knock!
  Who's there?
Mecca.
  Mecca who?
Mecca more noise and I'll go deaf!

Knock-knock!
   Who's there?
Navajo.
   Navajo who?
You'll Navajo until you try.

   Knock-knock
      Who's there?
   Nuisance.
      Nuisance who?
   This door nuisance I was here last?

      Knock-knock!
         Who's there?
      Odyssey.
         Odyssey who?
      Odyssey the new movie.

         Knock-knock!
            Who's there?
         Orange juice.
            Orange juice who?
         Orange juice coming with me?

Knock-knock!
   Who's there?
Osborn.
   Osborn who?
Osborn in a hospital, where were you born?

Knock-knock!
  Who's there?
Pharaoh.
  Pharaoh who?
Pharoah the yellow
brick road.

Knock-knock!
  Who's there?
Phyllis.
  Phyllis who?
Phyllis pitcher up with
lemonade.

Knock-knock!
  Who's there?
Pooch and Jimmy.
  Pooch and Jimmy who?
Pooch your arms around me and Jimmy a kiss!

Knock-knock!
  Who's there?
Roland.
  Roland who?
Roland in the mud will
make you dirty.

Knock-knock!
  Who's there?
Saliva.
  Saliva who?
Saliva the party. Let's
dance.

Knock-knock!
  Who's there?
Senior.
  Senior who?
Senior through the window so I know you're there!

Knock-knock!
  Who's there?
Sun Bear.
  Sun Bear who?
"Sun Bear over the rainbow. . ."

Knock-knock!
  Who's there?
Toulouse.
  Toulouse who?
Toulouse ten pounds of fat,
I have to exercise every day.

Knock-knock!
  Who's there?
Victor.
  Victor who?
Victor his pants climbing
the fence.

9. Crazy Careers!

What does a messy flea need?
A lousekeeper.

SALESPERSON: I'm calling because our company replaced your windows with weather-tight windows a year ago and we haven't received a single payment.

CUSTOMER: But you said the windows would pay for themselves in 12 months.

Why does Superman wear such big shoes?
  Because of his amazing feets!

What's red and blue, drowsy, and flies round the world?
  Stuporman!

JOE: Did you know that cats make the best reporters?
MOE: That's mews to me.

What does the postman deliver to vampires?
  Fang mail.

What was the first thing the lumberjack did when he bought a computer?
  He logged on.

One day a man walked into a barbershop wearing headphones. "Give me a trim," he said to the barber, "but don't take my headphones off or I'll die."

As the barber began to cut the man's hair, he realized the headphones were in the way and took them off. A few moments later, the man slumped to the floor dead.

Picking up the headphones, the barber put them to his ear and heard a voice saying, "Breathe in, breathe out, breathe in, breathe out..."

What's the scariest thing about flying Zombie Airlines?

The fright attendants.

A truck driver named Horace was driving along the freeway when he saw a sign, "Low Bridge Ahead." Thinking his truck could easily make it, Horace drove under the bridge and got stuck. Soon the other cars were honking their horns and shouting at Horace. Before long, a cop arrived and smiled at Horace's predicament. "Well, what's the problem? A little stuck, huh?" said the cop.

Thinking quickly, Horace grinned and replied, "No, I didn't get stuck. I was delivering this bridge and ran out of gas."

Because of the dangers of space travel, NASA decided to use robots as astronauts. Two robots began training for the space program. To test their readiness they had to parachute from an airplane, land, then ride a bicycle twenty miles back to NASA.

When it came time for the jump, both robots vaulted out of the plane and pulled their ripcords, but nothing happened. They pulled the emergency chute, but still nothing happened. As they whizzed to the ground, the first robot said to the second, "You know, I bet there won't be any bicycles waiting for us either."

A postal worker delivering a package knocked on the door of a house. A high-pitched voice said, "Come in."

Stepping inside, the postal worker suddenly found himself cornered by the biggest, most ferocious-looking dog he'd ever seen.

"Please!" called the postal worker. "Please call your dog off!"

"Come in!" repeated the voice.

As the dog got closer and closer, its teeth bared and ready to pounce, the postal worker felt the sweat pouring off his brow. "Hey, lady, please call your dog off right now!" the postal worker repeated.

"Come in," said the voice again.

Finally, the postal worker crept into the living room with the dog still at his heels and saw a parrot in a cage. "Come in!" squawked the parrot again.

"You stupid bird!" said the frightened postal worker. "Don't you know anything besides 'Come in'?"

"Squawk!" said the bird. "Sic him!"

10. Tasty Tickles!

How many dweebs does it take to make a batch of chocolate chip cookies?

100—one to stir and 99 to peel the M&Ms.

What's white and fluffy and beats its chest?

A meringue-utan.

What's the official hot dog of the Academy Awards?

Oscar Mayer.

BETTY: How do you make a hot dog stand?
NETTIE: First you steal its chair.

At an all-you-can-eat restaurant Joey came back to the table, his plate full for the fifth time.

"Joey!" exclaimed his mother. "Doesn't it embarrass you that people have seen you go up to the buffet table five times?"

"Not a bit," said Joey, "I just tell them I'm filling up the plate for you!"

On what day do spiders eat the most?
Flyday!

On what day do Internet freaks eat the most?
Webs-day.

Two absent-minded professors were watching TV one night. "How about a dish of ice cream?" said the first professor.

"Sounds good," replied the second professor. "I'll write it down so you won't forget."

"Don't worry, I won't forget," replied the first professor.

"But I want chocolate syrup and nuts on it."

"How could I forget that?"

A few minutes later the first professor returned with a plate of bacon and eggs.

"See, I knew I should have written it down," said the second professor. "You forgot the buttered toast!"

Where would you never see a vegetarian?
   At a meat-ing.

Why is a moon rock tastier than a meatball?
   Because it's a little meteor (meatier).

What's Godzilla's favorite big sandwich?
   Peanut butter and deli.

What would you get if you crossed a tangerine and a lion?
   An orange that nobody picks on.

LEMONS AND ORANGES AND GRAPES, OH MY!!

What would you get if you crossed a lion with crushed ice?
   A man-eating Slurpee!

Two bananas sat on the beach sunning themselves. After a while one banana got up and left. Why did she leave?

She was starting to peel.

What do you call a snake that drinks too much coffee?

A hyper-viper!

JEN: I have to stop eating so much spaghetti.
LEN: Why?
JEN: I went to the doctor and he said my blood type is Marinara.

What did the skeleton order at the restaurant?

Spare ribs.

What else did the skeleton order at the restaurant?

A glass of Coke and a mop.

What's long and orange and flies at the speed of sound?

A jet-propelled carrot.

What's the difference between the sun and a loaf of bread?

One rises from the East and the other from the yeast!

Lenny and Benny were walking their dogs when they decided to stop at a restaurant for a bite.

"But we're not allowed inside with pets," said Lenny, who owned a Chihuahua.

"Just watch and do what I do," said Benny.

When they arrived at the restaurant, Benny put on a pair of dark sunglasses and went inside.

"You can't come in here with a dog," said the hostess.

"But he's a guide dog," said Benny, pointing to his Doberman pinscher.

"Oh, right, sorry," said the hostess. "Please take a seat."

Next, Lenny put his dark glasses on and stepped inside with his dog.

"You can't come in here with a Chihuahua," said the hostess to Lenny.

"Oh, no!" said Lenny, "They gave me a Chihuahua?"

What breakfast cereal would you get if you crossed a cow with a baby's diaper?
Cream of Wet.

What do computer programmers like to eat for breakfast?
Ram & eggs.

When Willie tried to get a table in the restaurant, the hostess turned him away. "I'm sorry, sir, but you must wear a tie in our restaurant."

"But I don't have a tie," said Willie.

"Then you cannot dine at our restaurant," insisted the hostess.

Returning to his car, Willie got an idea. Pulling the jumper cables from his trunk, he managed to fashion them into a huge bow.

"Well?" said Willie to the hostess as he showed off his jumper cable tie.

"Well, all right," said the hostess. "You can come in—just don't start anything."

What sport do turkey chefs play?
Baste-ball.

What is the Abominable Snowman's favorite pasta?
Spag-yeti.

Where do hungry people go on vacation?
Snack-apulco.

"I can't figure out this jigsaw puzzle!" said the absent-minded professor to his wife.

"What kind of puzzle is it?" asked the wife.

"Well, there's a rooster on the box and it has a thousand pieces inside. It's so confusing I don't know where to start."

"It's all right, dear," said the professor's wife reassuringly. "Just put the Corn Flakes back in the box and go to bed."

SCIENTIST 1: I cloned a French chef with a zombie.
SCIENTIST 2: Are you happy with the results?
SCIENTIST 1: No, he gives me the crepes.

Knock-knock!
  Who's there?
Dishes.
  Dishes who?
Dishes the last joke!
the end—

Index

INDEX